MARIE
CURIE

What Made Them Great

Mary Montgomery

Illustrated by Severino Baraldi

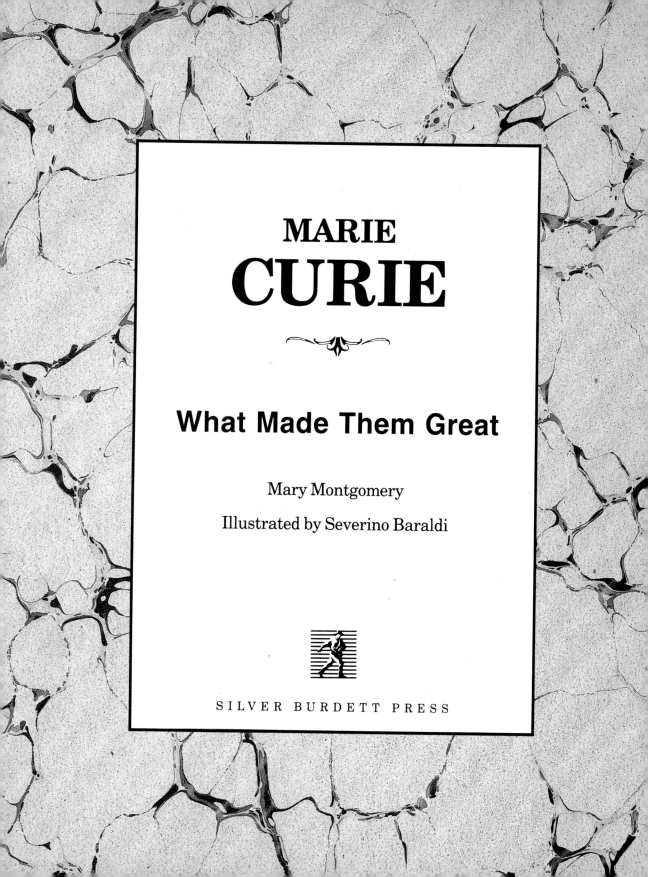

SILVER BURDETT PRESS

MARIE
CURIE

What Made Them Great

ACKNOWLEDGMENTS

Project Editor: Emily Easton (Silver Burdett Press)

Adapted and reformatted from the original by
Kirchoff/Wohlberg, Inc.

Project Director: John R. Whitman
Graphics Coordinator: Jessica A. Kirchoff
Production Coordinator: Marianne Hile

Library of Congress Cataloging-in-Publication Data

Montgomery, Mary Ann, 1931–
    Marie Curie/Mary Montgomery; illustrated by Severino Baraldi.
    p. cm.—[FROM SERIES: What Made Them Great]

Adaptation of: Marie Curie/Marina Montemayer; translated by Angela Ruiz.
    [FROM SERIES: Why They Became Famous]
    Includes bibliographical references.
Summary: A biography of the Polish-born scientist who, with her husband Pierre, was awarded a
    1903 Nobel Prize for discovering radium.
1. Curie, Marie, 1867-1934—Juvenile literature. 2. Chemists—Poland—Biography—Juvenile
    literature. [1. Curie, Marie, 1867-1934. 2. Chemists.] I. Baraldi, Severino, ill. II. Montemayer,
    Marina. Perché Sono Diventati Famosi, Marie Curie. III. Title. IV. Series.

| QD22.C8M66 1990 | 540.92—dc20 | [B] | [92] | 89-77113 | CIP | AC |

© Fabbri Editori S.p.A., Milan 1981
Translated into English by Angela Ruiz for Silver Burdett Press
from Perché Sono Diventati Famosi: Marie Curie
First published in Italy in 1981 by Fabbri Editori S.p.A., Milan

10 9 8 7 6 5 4 3 2 1 (Library Binding)
10 9 8 7 6 5 4 3 2 1 (Softcover)

ISBN 0-382-09981-8 (Library Binding)
ISBN 0-382-24006-5 (Softcover)

TABLE OF CONTENTS

Eager to Learn

Bronya Sklodowska ran to her mother. She buried her face in her mother's lap. A feeling of shame washed over her. She wished that the ground would open and swallow her up. Her little sister Manya, only four years old, was reading from a book that was too hard for Bronya.

How was that possible? Bronya was seven years old and already in school. But she could not read half as well as her baby sister. It was humiliating to Bronya.

"How shameful, Bronya!" she thought to herself. How would she ever find the courage to lift up her head again?

Manya Sklodowska was the youngest of five children. She was born in the city of Warsaw in Poland, on November 7, 1867. The Sklodowskas were a warm and loving family. In addition to Manya and

Bronya, there were two more sisters—Zosia and Hela. There was also a brother named Joseph.

As Manya grew up, she watched and listened and learned from her older brother and sisters. One day, she noticed Bronya cutting letters of the alphabet out of paper. Bronya was struggling to figure something out. To Manya, it looked like an exciting game. She wanted to play, too. Soon Manya realized that each of the letters had a different name. Each one even had its own sound. This discovery delighted Manya.

In no time at all, Manya could tell the vowels from the consonants. Then she figured out how to put them together to make words. And so, step by step, Manya learned to read.

Then came the day when she heard Bronya reading out loud from a schoolbook. When Bronya began to stumble over some of the words, Manya was eager to help. In her sweet, clear voice, she raced through the page that was giving Bronya trouble.

Manya was amazed when Bronya burst into tears. Why was her sister hiding her face in Mama's lap? Why was she upset? Manya raised her eyes from the book. She looked around, bewildered. She had only wanted to help Bronya. Had she done something wrong? She glanced at her father. He was trying hard not to smile. He even looked rather pleased. And though Mrs. Sklodowska was busy comforting Bronya, she did not seem angry at Manya, either. Quite the opposite; she seemed happy.

Manya was relieved. She remembered something that her father had once said. A thirst for knowledge, he had told her, was extremely important. She went on with her reading.

Manya's father was a professor. He taught mathematics and physics. Before Manya was born, her mother also had been a teacher. But after Manya was born, Mrs. Sklodowska had become ill. She had tuberculosis. At that time, there was no sure cure for the disease. The medicines she was taking seemed to do little good. Each day, she seemed to be weaker and weaker.

Mrs. Sklodowska dried Bronya's tears. Then she put Manya to sleep. She tucked in the child's sheets. She longed to kiss her daughter. But she dared not. Tuberculosis was catching. The doctors had warned Manya's mother to be careful about kissing the children. Instead, Mrs. Sklodowska bent over and stroked her child's hair. Manya's hair felt as soft as silk.

As Manya was sinking into sleep, she murmured, "Mother, I love you very much."

Mrs. Sklodowska smiled. "Sleep and dream of wonderful things, Manya," she whispered.

And Manya did. She dreamed of a wonderful place she sometimes went to in the countryside.

The Sklodowskas were city people, but they had many relatives who lived in the country. Manya loved visiting her cousins on their farm in the mountains.

How different everything was on the farm. There, Manya would see all kinds of animals. Gentle cows gave good rich milk that her aunt made into sweet-smelling butter. Especially exciting to Manya were the horses with their shiny hair. Often, she was allowed to ride on the smallest one.

The fresh mountain air gave Manya such a good appetite. Her mouth watered when she smelled bread, piping hot from the oven. Her eyes grew round over the sight and smell of fragrant cheeses and spicy sausages and a golden goose stuffed with honey. Back home, she could still remember how good they tasted.

Life in Warsaw was quite different. It was hard to recall when a stuffed goose had last appeared on the Sklodowskas' table. The professor's modest salary had to feed seven people.

There were a great many other expenses, too. Mrs. Sklodowska's medicine was expensive. The children had to be sent to school. That was costly. They needed nice clothing. It was a struggle to dress four daughters. To save money, the girls wore their dresses for as long as possible. How different those dresses were from the colorful ones worn by her cousins in the mountains.

Even though the Sklodowskas were far from well off, Manya was a happy little girl. She loved her family very much, and they loved her. There was a wonderful warm feeling in the household.

Manya could hardly wait for the day when she could go to school. At the age of five, she felt that time was standing still. She grew more and more impatient. All of the older children were allowed to attend school. But the Sklodowskas tutored their youngest child at home. This arrangement did not please Manya at all.

Actually, her parents did not know what to make of Manya. Each one of their children was extremely intelligent. But it was clear that little Manya was the brightest of them all. Indeed, she was special in many ways. She was a beautiful little girl. She had a remarkable memory. And she took enormous pleasure in learning.

After careful thought, the Sklodowskas made an unusual decision. They decided that it would be a mistake to push Manya's education. If they encouraged her studies, she might advance much too quickly. Then, she surely would be bored by the time she entered school. Best not to discuss too many grown-up ideas in front of her, they said to each other. And they also tried to stop her from reading.

However, Manya could not be stopped. Her father's studio was filled with books. The bookcases were jammed with old and new volumes. Some had pictures, and others had none. Some were bound in expensive leather, and others looked quite ordinary. To Manya, all of them were wonderful.

"Who knows why Mother and Father don't want me to have books!" she thought.

Every day, Manya watched for her chance. When nobody was paying attention, she would slip into her father's studio. She leafed through the many books there. They were about every subject— mathematics, physics, natural science, history, geography, literature, philosophy, chemistry, and sociology. They all fascinated Manya, and she read everything.

The studio was a simple room. It did not have luxurious furnishings. But for Manya, its books opened a window to a rich, bright world. She spent many hours reading. Of course, some of the books were much too difficult for her. She had trouble understanding the words. But she never allowed this to discourage her. Every day, she learned new words and discovered new ideas.

Sometimes, she got caught reading in the studio. Her father would come in and surprise her. Often, he found her with a book that was bigger than she was. However, he did not have the heart to scold her. Secretly, he felt proud of his daughter. Didn't he always tell his children that learning was the most important thing in life? This was his belief. Little Manya understood. She seemed to have a strong eagerness to learn. And her eagerness was matched by her determination.

One day, when Manya went into the studio to find a book, she happened to glance at her father's table. An experiment had been set up. One of the test tubes caught her attention. She climbed up on a chair to get a better look.

She picked up the test tube and held it up to the light. The tube was filled with a clear liquid. It gave off a strange reflection. Manya's curiosity was stirred. What could this be? she wondered. Puzzled, she put the test tube back in its place. She was careful not to spill anything. The professor would be terribly upset if she ruined one of his experiments.

Manya's father often locked himself in his studio and worked. Manya imagined him fussing with the test tubes. When he finally came out, he would look tired but happy. How marvelous science was, Manya thought. It must be the best fun in the world.

"When I grow up," she decided, "I'll do the same thing as Papa."

She made a promise to herself. She would study very hard. Then, someday, she would be just as smart as the professor.

"And even smarter!" she vowed.

School at Last

Finally, the day arrived when Manya went to school. Unfortunately, it was not quite as wonderful as she had expected. And sometimes it could be downright unpleasant. Growing up in Warsaw in the 1870s was difficult. Much of Poland had been conquered by Russia. Freedom seemed to have vanished. The Polish people hated living under Russian rule. They longed to drive out the invaders. Their greatest hope was to win back their liberty.

The Russians did their best to discourage such ideas. It was forbidden to speak Polish in the classroom. All the teachers and students had to learn to speak and read Russian. The Russian czar also had outlawed all books about the history of Poland. The children could not learn about their national heroes, either.

The situation was tragic. It was also extremely dangerous. Those who disobeyed the laws could be thrown into prison. Even worse, there was the risk of being sent away to a Russian labor camp in Siberia. As a result, there was always an atmosphere of fear in the classroom.

To make sure that no laws were being broken, the czar sent Russian inspectors around to the Polish schools. These men traveled from class to class, checking up on the teachers and the children.

In each classroom, the inspector would ask questions. The children were expected to answer in perfect Russian. They had to stand up tall, like soldiers. Anyone who smiled was sure to be scolded severely.

It is not surprising that the children felt sick with fear. They could not afford to give a wrong answer or make a mistake in Russian grammar. Above all, there could not be the slightest hint of disrespect for the inspector. That would mean trouble for their teachers as well as for their parents.

On the days when the inspector was due to arrive, Manya wished that she could stay at home. The teacher often called on her to recite for the inspector. It was natural for the teacher to pick Manya. She was the brightest student in the class. Learning Russian had been easy for her. It was not long before she could speak, read, and write the language perfectly. Still, the inspector's visit was a terrible ordeal for Manya. She hated having to show off her talents to an oppressor of her people.

One day, the inspector appeared and the room grew quiet. Manya's teacher looked a little scared. The inspector wore a blue uniform. Through his thick glasses, he stared coldly at the children. Everyone sat still, trying hard not to fidget.

The teacher called Manya's name. She was to begin reciting the day's lesson out loud. Manya rose to her feet. The expression on her face was solemn. She focused her eyes on the wall and began to speak. At first she recited in a very soft voice. As she gained confidence, her voice became stronger.

The inspector stared at Manya. There was no sign that he liked the recitation or that he disliked it. His expression was a blank. He just stood there, listening silently. Occasionally, he would lift one of his hands. The children watched as he stroked the tiny beard on his chin.

Abruptly, the inspector turned his back. Without uttering a word, he stalked out of the room. Everyone could hear him moving on to the next class. After he was gone, Manya could not remain silent. Her feelings burst out.

Running to the teacher, she cried, "Why? Why aren't we free from the terrible czar? When will our country belong to the Poles again?"

The teacher wrapped her arms around Manya. There was little that she could say. But she tried her best to offer a few words of comfort.

"That day will come," she promised. "I hope it will be soon."

But Manya could not forget the eyes of the Russian inspector. As he silently left the classroom, he had glanced back at Manya. His look was one of displeasure. It almost seemed as if the girl's intelligence annoyed him. She never gave a wrong answer. That meant there was nothing to complain about to the director of the school or to the girl's parents.

During this time, Professor Sklodowska was in trouble with the authorities at his school. He had tried to defend a student who had been unfairly punished. The case came to the attention of the czar's officers. The director of the school where the professor taught grew nervous. It would be a mistake to offend the Russians. To prevent possible problems, the director decided to fire Professor Sklodowska.

Manya's father had done a courageous deed. But now he was without a job. He wondered how he could make ends meet. The situation was desperate. The family moved to a cheaper house. They rented rooms to students who paid a monthly charge. With the house full of boarders, the peace and quiet of earlier years became a memory.

The professor had a small amount of money saved. But this money was being set aside for the education of his children. To support his family, the professor was forced to become a tutor. He took private students. There seemed to be no other choice. At the same time, he continued to look for additional ways to make money.

Professor Sklodowska learned that his brother-in-law was installing a steam mill. This mill looked as if it would be very profitable. It meant taking a risk, but Manya's father decided to invest part of his savings in his brother-in-law's business.

Unfortunately, the mill failed, and the money for the children's education was lost. Once again, the professor was practically ruined.

Then another more terrible disaster struck. One of the students who lived with the Sklodowskas became sick. The student had a terrible headache. He also was running a very high fever. A doctor was called. The student had typhus, a contagious disease that could cause death.

Almost immediately, both Bronya and Zosia came down with typhus. Anguish gripped the Sklodowska house. Those were dreadful days.

Weeks went by. Slowly the student began to get well. Bronya, too, recovered little by little. Only Zosia failed to improve. Mr. and Mrs. Sklodowska watched her toss in bed, unable to fight off the fever and the illness. Nothing could save her. Zosia was just fourteen years old when she died.

The family was inconsolable. Manya simply could not believe that her sister was gone. It was too terrible to understand.

For a long time to come, Manya could still hear her sister's sweet voice. She even imagined that she could see Zosia sewing in the parlor. Gradually, these visions faded. She accepted the fact that Zosia would never return.

After Zosia's death, Mrs. Sklodowska seemed to grow older suddenly. She always looked tired. Once her hair had been spectacular—long, thick, and golden brown. She had worn it in a large bun, as was the fashion in those years. But, almost overnight, her hair turned the color of silver. Her lovely oval face grew thin and pale.

It is very likely that the death of her daughter affected her health. No longer did she have the strength to fight her own illness. The tuberculosis grew worse. Mrs. Sklodowska became thinner. Each day she seemed to cough more and more.

Finally, there came a morning when Mrs. Sklodowska was too weak to get out of bed.

It was clear that the end was drawing near. Her illness had reached its final stages. There was nothing more that could be done. Manya's mother understood that she was going to die soon. Perhaps only a few days remained. Perhaps she had only a few hours left. She accepted her fate calmly.

But Manya was far from resigned. She was hoping for a miracle. She prayed as she had never prayed before. Sadly, it was of no use. Her mother continued to fail.

Manya kept watch by her mother's bedside. "Mother," she would call out softly. "Mother, don't leave us." She squeezed her mother's cold hand.

Mrs. Sklodowska smiled at her.

"Darling," she said to her daughter, "I must go. I am going to be with Zosia."

She urged Manya not to be afraid. Even though she would not see Manya again, she would always be with her in spirit.

Then, she turned her face toward her husband. "My dear," she whispered, "I leave them with you. Now you will be both father and mother to them."

A moment later she was silent.

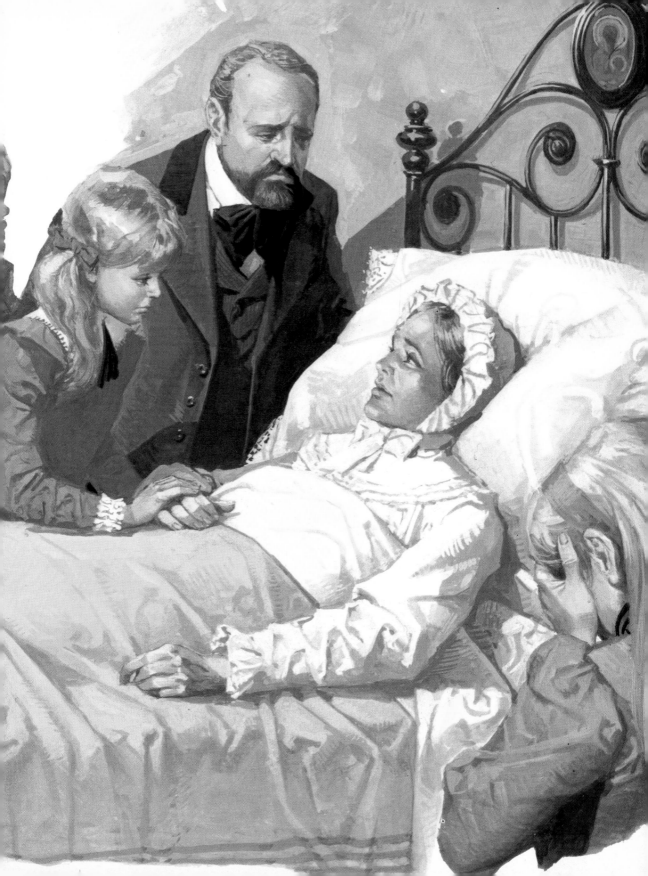

"Congratulations, Manya!"

t was graduation day at Manya's school. Excited friends and classmates crowded around her. "Congratulations, Manya!" someone called out. "You've done well! We're proud of you!"

Everybody tried to hug her. They told her how pleased and proud of her they felt. And, of course, they clamored to see the gold medal that she had just won.

Manya's cheeks began to turn bright pink. All this attention was making her feel embarrassed. She clutched her diploma and her gold medal.

The years had sped by for Manya. It was now 1883. In spite of her worries about her family, she had done extremely well in school. She was at the top of her class.

Her beloved mother's death had been difficult to accept. For a long while, the house seemed empty. In their grief, the children drew closer to one another. As he had promised his wife, the professor became both father and mother to Hela, Joseph, Bronya, and Manya. He made sure to spend as much time with them as he could. Sometimes this was not easy, because he had to work so hard.

As the years passed, the professor depended more and more on his children. His main joy in life became his family. But the shock of losing his wife never really wore off. His sadness could be read on his face. His hair and beard had turned white.

At the ceremony on Manya's graduation day, the professor felt very happy. "Dear daughter," he said, "I am very proud of you. If your poor mother were here, she would be so pleased."

Manya felt tears well up in her eyes.

Her father said, "You are a very dear daughter, and I consider myself a very fortunate father."

As he spoke, Manya watched her father's face. Suddenly, he seemed years and years younger to her. A bright light shone in his tired eyes. He looked confident. His smile was full of happiness. Seldom had Manya seen her father so content since Mrs. Sklodowska's death.

Little wonder that the professor rejoiced. All of his other children had completed secondary school. And now Manya, the youngest, was also graduating. What's more, she had won a gold medal for her achievements. A brilliant student, she had managed to graduate one year earlier than the other children her age. She was not yet sixteen.

At the graduation, Manya stayed at her father's side. She stood out from her classmates, who wore brightly colored dresses. Their hair was tied back with ribbons and bows. Unlike the other girls, Manya was dressed in black. She had no colored ribbons in her hair. The only decoration she wore was a rose pinned to her gown. In her best black dress, she looked like a dark swallow that had wandered by accident into a flock of hummingbirds.

Manya's graduation day was one of the most important days in her life. A long chain of successes lay in her future, of course. Graduation with honors was the first step. She was only fifteen, but already she had learned an important lesson—nothing comes without hard work. The years of grueling study were still fresh in her mind. To obtain that precious diploma, she had given up many hours of fun and good times.

When the ceremonies were over, Professor Sklodowska made an announcement. He said he had a surprise for Manya.

For a long while, he had been concerned about his youngest daughter. Suffering had caused her to grow up too quickly. She worked too hard. There was no denying that she was sweet and well mannered. But, in his opinion, she was too serious for her age. After all, she was still a child. It was a shame to miss the pleasures of childhood.

The professor stroked his white beard. "You have studied so hard that you are one year ahead," he said to Manya. "Now you deserve to have fun. You should be with boys and girls your own age."

Manya opened her mouth to argue. But her
father held up his hand. She was to spend a year
with her relatives who lived in the mountains. The
vacation was all arranged.

"I want you to enjoy yourself," he said firmly.

Leaving her family was upsetting. But
Manya's cousins were very affectionate and made
her feel happy and at home.

Living in the country was exciting. Manya
loved the holidays and the wonderful celebrations.
She wore colorful dresses like the villagers. Mouth-
watering platters of food were served. Manya spent
many evenings dancing. The musicians would strike
up a tune. To the strains of the fiddles, Manya would
whirl breathlessly around the floor.

The heavenly colors of spring in the mountains delighted Manya. She also loved summer, when the fields lay soft under the buttery sun. Then, at harvest time, the leaves blazed red and gold.

Perhaps best of all was winter. Manya and her cousins piled into sleighs and raced over the snow-covered fields. The sounds of laughter and sleigh bells rang out through the icy air.

Manya could not believe how fast the months flew by. Before she knew it, the year was over. It was time to go home to Warsaw.

The Road to Paris

Back in Warsaw, Manya began to teach poor women who were workers in a factory. These people had never been given the chance to attend school. The government of the czar tried to keep the Polish people ignorant. That way, the government could control them more easily.

Manya held secret classes in a plant with gray-painted walls. There were even bars on the windows. To Manya, the gloomy factory looked like a prison. The workers were obliged to put in ten or twelve and sometimes fourteen hours a day. What's more, they were treated badly and paid miserable wages.

The women workers were enthusiastic students. Manya did her best to answer their questions. She made sure to explain difficult subjects clearly. She even lent her pupils some books.

Once, she overheard two of the women talking. They were admiring Manya's patience. Even the slowest student was never scolded. One of the workers said, "Miss Sklodowska gives such good explanations. I've been able to understand everything."

Manya was not about to tell them that she felt a little afraid. She was pleased to know that she appeared confident. Before long, she was spending

most of her free time at the factory. The days in the country and the sleigh rides seemed far away.

Actually, Manya did not have much free time. She was busy making plans for her future. Manya's brother Joseph had begun to study medicine at the university. Manya and Bronya wanted to go there, too. However, this was impossible, because women were not allowed to study at the university.

If the two sisters wished to continue their education, they would have to leave Poland. But this, too, seemed unlikely to happen. Studying in a foreign land would require a great deal of money. Professor Sklodowska had none to give them. Indeed, their father was barely able to make ends meet at home. His savings had been spent on trying to cure his wife's tuberculosis and on his brother-in-law's steam mill.

The sisters realized that they would have to manage on their own. Bronya was twenty years old. Manya was only sixteen. Full of enthusiasm, the young women began to make plans. Bronya knew exactly what she wanted. It was to study medicine, like Joseph. Manya, however, was still undecided.

Their biggest problem was money. Without money, their ambitions would forever remain distant dreams. The unhappy truth was that they were penniless.

To earn their living, they decided to become teachers. Like their father, they would give lessons to private students. Of course, they were still very young and lacked the professor's years of experience. And they were women. They hoped these drawbacks could be overcome. After all, their education had been excellent. But to be on the safe side, they charged reasonable prices.

Without too much trouble, they managed to find a number of wealthy Warsaw families whose children needed tutoring. Manya taught arithmetic, geometry, and French.

As was the custom, lessons were conducted at the students' homes. Generally this meant traveling all over the city. Sometimes, the pupils lived miles away. Neither Manya nor Bronya minded. They were young and full of energy.

A year went by. Manya and Bronya were still racing from one end of Warsaw to the other. They taught a variety of subjects. Unfortunately, their pupils were disappointing. Unlike the factory women, they had little interest in learning. Mostly, they were lazy youngsters. They didn't pay attention. They talked back. There were occasions when Manya simply put on her hat and coat—and she quit.

One thing was clear to Manya. Although the sisters were working very hard, their earnings from tutoring were too small. It was impossible to save enough money to study abroad. At this rate, they would never achieve their goal.

There was no hurry for Manya, who was seventeen. But her sister had already turned twenty-one. Bronya hoped to attend the famous Sorbonne University in Paris, France. But she couldn't wait forever. Medical school took five years. Manya pondered how this dilemma could be solved.

Seated at her desk, she began to jot down some figures. Soon there were pages filled with numbers. She was busy making lists. How much money would a person need to live in Paris? How much for food and lodging? How much for tuition and books? She tried to think of everything. Even the cost of firewood was included.

When the figures were added up, the situation looked hopeless. All of their savings would barely pay for a one-way ticket to Paris and a year's expenses. And that was just for one person.

But, as always, Manya was determined. Soon the answer came to her. There was a way to send Bronya to the Sorbonne. It was simple. Manya would give up her private pupils. Instead, she would work as a governess for just one family. That meant she could live with her employers. There would be no expense for rent or food.

Excited, Manya hurried into the parlor to find her sister. As she explained the idea, Bronya listened quietly.

Manya said, "I can give you whatever I've saved so far. And then each week I could send you

almost my entire pay. What do you say?" She was smiling happily.

Bronya slowly rose from her chair and clasped her sister's hand. "Dear sister, I could never accept such a sacrifice."

But Manya would not take no for an answer. "Don't be silly," she chided. "It's the only way. And once you graduate and begin to earn money, you can help me."

Bronya had tears in her eyes. "You'll have to wait five years. It's not fair, Manya."

Manya shrugged. Bronya was the older one. It was only right that her turn should come first.

Persuading Bronya was not easy. Manya joked, "Think what fine work you'll do at the Sorbonne. And by the time I arrive, the Sklodowska name will be famous!"

With reluctance, Bronya finally accepted the plan. She left for Paris and the university she had dreamed of attending.

Manya found a position as a governess with a wealthy family. They lived some miles from Warsaw. Manya soon settled into her new life. She was to teach a girl named Andzia. Luckily, Andzia was a capable student and the lessons went well. Manya's employers were pleased. As time went by, they realized their good fortune in hiring her.

Everyone in the family behaved politely to Manya. However, they were standoffish. They did not consider her to be their equal. The fact was that Manya was their employee. Sometimes the young woman felt very lonely.

During Manya's first year with the family, she learned that there were many local children unable to read and write. She decided to organize a free school. Teaching in her spare time made her feel useful and less lonely.

The time that was left was devoted to her own studies. She read everything she could put her hands on. Practically every subject still interested her. Sometimes there were things that she did not understand. Then she would write to her father for an explanation.

During this period, Manya came to an important realization. The subjects that she enjoyed most of all were physics and mathematics.

A second and a third year went by. Manya continued to work and study. She saved as much of her salary as she could and sent it to Bronya.

By now, her employers had grown more friendly toward Manya. After dinner, they would invite her to chat or play chess.

One day, their oldest son, Casimir, came home on vacation. Handsome and polite, Casimir was a student in Warsaw. Suddenly, he began to take a great interest in Manya. For the first time, he realized that she was extremely pretty. What's more, she was unusually charming and intelligent.

In a short while, young Casimir fell in love with Manya. He could not conceal his feelings. Even though he barely knew Manya, he told his parents that he loved her. He announced that he planned to marry the young governess.

At first, Casimir's family was shocked. When their surprise wore off, they became angry. Of course Manya was lovely and sweet. But she had no money. What's more, she did not belong to their social class.

"She's only a governess," Casimir was told. Marrying a governess was impossible. It would disgrace the family.

Casimir backed down. No longer did he speak of love and marriage. Manya was an extremely proud young woman. She had taken Casimir seriously. She may have hoped to become his wife. Now, it was over. Her thoughts became bitter.

After this painful incident, the family grew less friendly. Life with them became unbearable for Manya. She would have liked to leave, but she needed the income.

Manya pictured the last time she had seen Warsaw. Its skies were gray and snowy. Her father and friends had gathered to say good-bye. Curled up in the corner of the coach, Manya had sadly watched the drifting snowflakes. A wave of homesickness swept over her now. She made up her mind to go home as soon as Andzia no longer needed her.

Manya....Marie

Shortly after her return to Warsaw, Manya received a surprising letter from Paris. Bronya wrote that she had met a Polish doctor there. They were to be married. Bronya would not need Manya's financial help any longer. Bronya

and her husband planned to live in Paris. How would Manya like to live with them and attend the Sorbonne?

The news delighted Manya. There was only one problem. How could she pay the tuition at the Sorbonne? With her goal so near, she was

determined to find a way. She did. She found work in the scientific laboratory of a cousin.

By September 1891, Manya had saved the amount she needed to study at the Sorbonne in Paris. She was ready to pack her belongings and leave. She was now twenty-four years old.

Manya boarded the train to France. It was a very long trip. Tired but happy, Manya barely noticed. Finally, the train pulled into the station at Paris. Her sister and brother-in-law were waiting on the platform. Manya flung herself into their arms.

Bronya could not stop talking. Manya, dazed, kept sweeping her eyes over the huge train station. It was one of the most exciting days of her life. She felt as if she were dreaming.

"How is Father?" Bronya asked. "What were his last words to you?"

"Oh, he advised me to do well," Manya said. "Poor Father. He's so lonely. He made me promise to return as soon as I graduate."

How wonderful it felt to be in the beautiful city of Paris. Under the many years of Russian rule, life in Poland had become dreary and lifeless. But here in France, the atmosphere was exactly the opposite. There was freedom. In Paris, people looked cheerful. They lived, studied, worked, and spoke as they pleased.

Everything about the city delighted Manya. Strolling through the streets, she felt like a small girl who had wandered into an amusement park. Like a wide-eyed tourist, she gaped at the famous monuments. She visited the historical sights. She loved to watch the boats moving up and down the river Seine. Paris was certainly a splendid city.

Not long after she arrived in Paris, Manya decided to change her name. It seemed that her classmates found "Manya" difficult to pronounce. So she translated her name into French. That is how Manya Sklodowska became Marie Sklodowska.

Even though Marie knew French, it was hard for her to understand her professors at the university. They spoke so fast! So the young Polish woman had to work to learn this foreign language even better.

There were other problems, as well, that were more difficult to solve. At the Sorbonne, Marie was a foreigner. She was not sure she would ever win the acceptance of the other students—or of her professors. She had changed her name. But she felt that, to the French, Miss Sklodowska would always be Polish.

Also, she was poor. Almost all her classmates came from well-to-do families. In the 1890s, Paris was the fashion capital of the world. The avenues were filled with elegant ladies and gentlemen in white gloves. The women wore stylish gowns and hats. The Parisian men looked dashing with their curled mustaches and starched collars.

Carrying her books under her arm, Marie would march briskly through the streets. But sometimes she could not help feeling out of place. Her dress was not at all fashionable. The hat on her head was plain and drab. Her shoes were always polished, but they were old and worn.

Marie also met with prejudice at the university because she was a woman. At that time, very few women attended the Sorbonne. They were regarded with suspicion by their male classmates. Professors also tended to prefer men students.

Marie was determined to rise above all these barriers. She wanted to win the confidence of her professors and classmates. But how? In order to succeed, she believed that she had to work harder than everyone else. Only superhuman accomplishments could overcome their prejudices, she decided.

Surprisingly, staying with Bronya and her husband was not helping Marie to succeed. Of course, her sister and brother-in-law were very kind to her. But there were difficulties.

For one thing, their home was located quite far from the Sorbonne. Marie spent a great deal of time traveling back and forth. Also, the doctor and his wife were fond of parties. Almost every night their friends would gather at their house to play music or cards.

Marie enjoyed parties, too, but not every night. When company arrived, she could not excuse herself and go to her room to do her work. It would have been impolite. To study, she had to wait until the guests went home.

Marie hardly ever got enough sleep. The oil lamp in her room burned later and later every night. There were so many things to learn and there was never enough time. She was not making enough progress. How could she concentrate in the home of her sister and her husband? She was worried.

Marie could not forget her father's last words as she was leaving Poland. "Try to do well," he had urged her. "Try to excel."

All that kept her going were the professor's words and the memory of her loved ones at home.

Eventually, she made up her mind. It was very painful, but there was no choice. She explained to her sister that she would have to move.

At first, Bronya was upset. She was sure that she must have offended Marie. What had she and her husband done wrong?

Marie hastened to apologize. It was not their fault, she insisted. They could not have been kinder or more generous to her. She felt grateful.

But didn't Bronya see? She needed to work harder for some of her courses. For years, Marie had been studying alone. At the Sorbonne, she had been dazzled by new ideas. Now she realized how little she actually knew. There were vast gaps in her education. It was important to fill those gaps as quickly as possible. But in order to do that, she must be able to work in peace and quiet.

"Bronya, please try to understand," she said.

Her sister smiled. "You're right, Marie," she sighed. "Your leaving makes me sad. But you must do what you think best. And please don't worry. I understand."

Marie found a room. It was located on the top floor of a building close to the university. The room was tiny. In winter, she froze. In summer, she sweltered. But the rent was very low. The idea of a room of her own filled her with hope. Now she could devote every minute to her studies.

The days were long and full. She spent her time studying and attending lectures. She also performed experiments in the physics lab. This busy schedule left no time for fun. Sometimes, she didn't bother to eat. Even preparing soup was too much trouble.

When winter came, she stayed late at the library. In that way, she was able to save money. Oil for her reading lamp was expensive. Besides, her cramped little room was freezing cold. Often she could not afford to buy firewood.

When the library closed, Marie hurried home to her cold attic room. Exhausted, she would fall on her cot and sleep a few hours. All too soon, it would be a new day and she would tramp back to the university.

In a few months, Marie had soared to the head of her class. Everyone could not help being impressed with her. It was true that her clothing looked funny and her shoes were patched. But her brilliance could not be overlooked. Bit by bit, Marie began to win the admiration of her professors and classmates.

There were no boyfriends in Marie's life. In her younger days, she had been open and friendly. Then had come her unhappy romance with Casimir. His parents' refusal to approve of her had humiliated her. She became shy around men.

At the Sorbonne, she believed that the young men did not find her attractive. She was convinced that she was too poor to interest them romantically.

During this period, she made only a few friends. Mostly, they were Polish students who talked about politics. Fervent patriots, they were determined that Poland should throw off the rule of the czar and become free again.

As her workload increased, Marie had little time for amusement. Now, she was more alone than ever. She slaved over her books and experiments. Her goal of graduating from the university drew closer. But the cost was high. Eyes ringed with fatigue, she grew pale and thin. Nevertheless, with her usual determination, she kept going.

First in Her Class

arie's brother proudly raised his glass in a salute. "Hurrah, dear sister," he cried. Around the dining-room table, the other members of the family and their friends lifted their glasses, too. They all called out toasts to Marie.

Marie smiled happily. She glanced around the table. School had ended for the year. Now it was the summer of 1893 and she was back home again. How she had missed her family and her native country! She reached for her glass and clinked it against her father's. For the first time in two years, she was in the mood to celebrate.

Marie had just passed her examinations. She had received a master's degree in physics. Much to her joy, she had graduated first in her class. Hard work had paid off.

Professor Sklodowska was deeply touched. He understood how much his daughter had struggled. Her success filled him with enormous pride. "Master of Physics," he kept saying. Then he leaned over to Marie and whispered, "Are you happy?"

"Of course, Father."

"And you really *did* excel, didn't you?"

Marie smiled. She had never forgotten her father's words of advice, as she had set out for Paris. "Try to excel," he had told her. And she had.

During the summer Marie thought about what she might do now. She wanted to return to the Sorbonne. Now that she had a degree in physics, she wanted to study mathematics. But once again, the problem was a lack of money.

Her family sympathized. But there was nothing they could do to assist her. "Your talent should not be wasted," lamented her brother.

Others agreed. One of Marie's friends was able to help. Without telling Marie, she convinced Polish officials that Marie should be given money to continue her studies. When Marie was offered a scholarship, she was astonished. She accepted with gratitude and returned to the Sorbonne in Paris.

After another year of study, she was awarded still another degree. This time it was in mathematics. Marie ranked second in her class. As soon as she was able, she paid back the scholarship money so that it could go to help another student.

While she was at the Sorbonne, Marie had begun work on projects that interested her. One of her teachers helped her find her first job. She was hired to do research by an organization called the Society for the Development of National Industry. She was to study the magnetic properties of different kinds of steel.

Marie needed space to set up her experiments. Her own room was too small. Even her science professor's laboratory could not hold all the instruments Marie needed. And she could not afford to pay very much to rent space.

One day, Marie was explaining her problem to Dr. Kovalski, a Polish scientist whom she knew. He thought for a few minutes. Then he said, "I may have a solution for you. A friend of mine has an extra room. Maybe he'll let you use it." The next day, Dr. Kovalski introduced Marie to Pierre Curie.

Pierre Curie was a brilliant French scientist. He had obtained his degree at an early age. Already he had made important discoveries with his brother Jacques, who was also a scientist. As a result, he had won many significant prizes in science. His special interest was testing the properties of crystals.

Pierre Curie and Marie Sklodowska were interested in each other from the very first moment they met. The tall, handsome Frenchman was able to offer Marie a room in which to set up her laboratory. Also, they got along splendidly. They shared so many interests. When Pierre asked if he might see her again, Marie agreed at once.

As the weeks went by, Marie and Pierre saw each other frequently. They would spend hours talking together. Both of them were devoted to science. Both felt happiest in a laboratory. As a couple, they seemed to be a perfect match.

Every day, Marie got to know Pierre better and appreciate him more. She was always eager to learn more about his experiments. In addition to his work with crystals, Pierre was doing research on magnetism. He hoped to discover new facts about the magnetic properties of different substances.

Marie encouraged Pierre to get his doctor's degree in physics. He did and, soon after graduation, he asked Marie to marry him.

The Marriage
of the Curies

Marie felt doubtful when
Pierre had first asked her
to marry him. She gave
his proposal a great deal of
thought. She loved him, but
she didn't know if she could
remain in France. All along,
she had planned to return
to Poland. She wanted to
live near her father. She had
promised him that she would.
Also, she wondered how
marriage would affect
her career.

For almost a whole
year, Marie could not make
up her mind. Pierre waited
anxiously for her decision.
He even suggested that they
move to Warsaw. To be with
Marie, he was willing to give
up everything—his work, his
parents and friends, his native

land. Marie knew she could never accept such a huge sacrifice for her sake.

Marie felt torn. Could she leave her father and her homeland forever? On the other hand, her feelings for Pierre kept growing. How could she stand to be away from the man she loved? It was a difficult choice.

Finally, she realized that she must marry Pierre. They would live in France. At the time, Marie was twenty-eight. Pierre was thirty-six.

In 1895, Marie and Pierre were married. It was a cloudless summer day in July. Friends and relatives gathered in the garden of the house where Pierre had been born.

Marie insisted on having a simple wedding. Indeed, there was no choice. Both she and Pierre were too poor to be married in style. This left Marie with a problem: a traditional wedding dress was very costly. And it could be worn only once. What could she wear for her wedding? What could she afford?

Marie was a practical woman. Why not select an ordinary dress? she began to think. Then it could be worn on other occasions. In the end, she chose a pretty but simple blue suit. With the suit, she wore a blue-striped blouse.

After the ceremony, a few friends and relatives gathered at the house of Pierre's parents. Of course, Bronya and her husband were there.

Professor Sklodowska arrived from Warsaw. He was accompanied by Marie's other sister, Hela. Unfortunately Joseph could not be there, but he sent an affectionate letter.

Pierre and Marie stood side by side in the cool and shady garden. All the flowers were in bloom. The air smelled sweet and delicious.

"Long live the newlyweds!" someone called out.

Beaming with happiness, the bride and groom accepted the congratulations of their guests.

The Curies had little money. But they were rich in enthusiasm and plans for the future.

First, Marie and Pierre were determined to have a honeymoon trip. With the money they had received as wedding gifts, they bought two bicycles. Shortly after the wedding, they climbed on their shiny, brand-new bicycles and rode off on a leisurely tour through the French countryside. There they were—two scientists. One was French, the other was Polish. They had met, fallen in love, and married. They felt like the happiest couple in the world.

All during the month of August, Marie and Pierre spent the days riding from town to town. Their troubles were left behind. Their work, the lab, their lack of money—all were forgotten for a while.

The weather turned out to be perfect. To show his wife the beauty of her new country pleased Pierre very much. And Marie loved the peace and beauty of nature. Exploring the country lanes, they felt as free as two small children.

Neither of them would ever forget the happiness of that trip. There was so much to see: thick, dark forests, meadows carpeted with wildflowers, cool, silvery brooks.

Time did not exist for them. Whenever they came to an interesting sight, they stopped and got off their bicycles. For hours, they would lose

themselves in gazing at a bird's nest. Or they
gawked at sunsets, watched cows grazing in the
fields, stared at flowers and ripening fruit and blue
skies. In the villages, they stayed at humble inns
and dined on delicious country cooking.

They wished the trip would never be over.
Finally, however, the summer drew to an end. It was
time to ride their bicycles back to Paris. There was
important work waiting to be done.

In October, they rented a three-room apartment overlooking a garden. Their furnishings were very few. Pierre's father offered them money. He even offered to buy them furniture for their house. The couple refused. They preferred to manage for themselves, even if it meant strict budgeting.

Pierre's salary as a professor was not large. Marie was continuing her studies. Her goal was to pass certain exams so that she, too, could teach. Then she would have an income to add to the family budget.

Marie was studying to earn a doctor's degree. This involved choosing a subject that she could research. It had to be a new topic. She had to find a subject about which nothing was yet known. After discovering new facts, she would write a lengthy report called a thesis. Then she would receive a doctor's degree. After that, she would deserve to be called "doctor."

In addition to her studies, Marie was expected to run the household. Where would she find the time? she wondered. Each of her extra responsibilities ate up precious hours.

She decided to treat the problem in a scientific manner. She would order her time—so many hours for study, so many hours for household chores. This idea seemed to work.

Just at this time, Marie became interested in the work of a French scientist, Dr. Henri Becquerel.

Becquerel had been experimenting with a metal called uranium. He discovered that uranium ore gives off invisible rays of radiation. These rays were similar to X rays. Even though Dr. Becquerel had presented his ideas to the French Scientific Academy, there were many questions that he had not answered.

What could be causing the rays? What were the effects of the radiation? Were they dangerous? Like many other scientists, the Curies were excited by Becquerel's research.

Marie decided to choose radiation as the subject of her research for her doctor's degree. It was an interesting subject. She would test materials that gave off radiation. She felt that she would be able to find the answers to Becquerel's questions.

If Marie succeeded, she would gain a great deal. She would become a professor. And, of course, she also would make an important contribution to science.

Early in 1897, Marie realized that she was expecting a baby. Although the Curies wanted children, Marie began to worry. Being a mother was a very big challenge. Of course, so was physics. Marie was not sure that she could manage the demands of both.

Despite her worries, Marie's activities during the pregnancy changed very little. She continued to work and study, just as hard as usual.

Pierre's mother felt great affection for her daughter-in-law. For a time, Pierre's mother came to live with them, to help Marie with the housework.

In September 1897, Marie gave birth to a daughter. The Curies named her Irène.

After nearly two years of marriage, Marie and Pierre still owned very little. Their apartment did not contain much besides a table, two chairs, and a bed. But now a new piece of furniture was added. The Curies bought a beautiful and comfortable cradle for the newest member of the family.

Baby Irène was healthy and beautiful. But like all babies, she needed constant attention. Marie had to work even harder. She cared for the house and her child, and did her studies. But it became impossible for Marie to keep up with her experiments. She could not leave little Irène in her cradle, while she went off to the Sorbonne to work. However, if she ever hoped to become a professor, she must continue her study of radiation.

Marie would be forced to find a solution. Her income would be important to the family. Whenever she had to go to the lab, she hired a nurse to care for Irène.

The Nobel Prize

arie's lab was small and freezing cold. It was really only a storeroom in a tumbledown shed. But nothing could dampen Marie's enthusiasm. The important thing was that she had a laboratory of her own. The delicate instruments needed for her experiments were set up.

During the weeks that followed, Marie tested many kinds of minerals. Some contained small amounts of uranium. These, she discovered, gave forth weak rays. Other minerals contained more uranium. They gave off much stronger rays. To Marie, it seemed that uranium was the key. The more uranium, the more powerful the rays.

Eventually, Marie became interested in thorium. Like uranium, thorium was a metallic element. It had been discovered only recently. And like uranium, thorium gave off strong bursts of radiation. It, too, was radioactive.

There were three minerals that contained both uranium and thorium. They were black pitchblende, green chalcocite, and yellow uraninite. Marie measured the amount of radioactivity in each of these minerals. To her surprise, they were all more radioactive than pure uranium. How was that possible? She wondered if she had made a mistake.

After more tests, she decided that the three minerals must contain something else—something more than uranium and thorium. They must contain something that she knew nothing about. The "something else" might account for the strong radioactivity. Now she had to prove her idea. Pierre put aside his own work in order to help Marie hunt for the puzzling new element.

Day after day they toiled. They experimented with pitchblende, which is made up of numerous elements. One by one, they had to eliminate each of the elements they knew, until only the mysterious "something else" was left. Finally, they discovered that the pitchblende contained not one, but two new elements.

In July 1898, they were able to identify one of the mystery elements. What should they call their important discovery? In honor of her native land, Marie named the new element "polonium."

Tired but happy after their discovery, the Curies took a vacation. They rode through the countryside on their bicycles. When they returned, they felt refreshed and eager to return to work. Their search was not over yet. There was that second mysterious radioactive element to locate.

Four months later, they discovered the element radium. In Latin, radium means "ray."

The Curies' latest discovery did not mean that their work was over. Now it was necessary to explain the effects of radiation. Three more years of research were before them. By 1902, they had the answers to their questions.

Marie eagerly shared the news of the discoveries with her family. Bronya and her husband had returned to Poland, where they built a hospital. Marie often exchanged letters with them.

Professor Sklodowska also took a keen interest in the Curies' work. But he did not live to see the importance of their discovery. In 1902, he became sick. When Marie heard the news, she went to Warsaw at once. But her father died before she arrived.

The year 1902 had started out well. But at the end, several unhappy events had taken place. Her father's death shattered Marie. She had never really forgiven herself for leaving Poland and her father. Also, Marie had another child. But the baby died shortly after it was born.

Other misfortunes put a strain on the family. For a long while, Pierre had wanted to become a lecturer in mineralogy at the Sorbonne. But the university offered the job to another professor. Pierre was hurt by this, and when the university wanted to award him the Legion of Honor, Pierre refused to accept the prize.

The following year turned out to be much brighter. In 1903, Marie finally presented her discoveries to the Sorbonne. She received her

doctor's degree and became a physics professor. But her work was so important that it brought Marie much more than a degree. It brought both the Curies to the attention of the entire scientific world. News of their discoveries had spread quickly. Many prizes, diplomas, and medals were awarded to the couple.

Then, at the end of 1903, came the greatest honor of all. Marie and Pierre Curie won the Nobel Prize in physics. This is the highest award that a physicist can win. It was awarded to them for their discovery of radioactivity.

Overnight, the Curies became world famous. They found themselves in the spotlight. Marie, in particular, caught the fancy of the public. Few women in all of history had achieved as much as she.

Along with the Nobel Prize came a large cash award. For the first time in their lives, the Curies were free from financial worries. However, they chose not to keep all the money. They gave some of it to Bronya and her husband for their hospital. Another portion was donated to aid the cause of Polish liberty.

After winning the Nobel Prize, the Curies were able to give up teaching. It became possible for them to devote all their time to research. The following year, the Curies had another child, Eve. Marie was very happy.

The years of poverty were over.

A Life Dedicated
to Science

I t was a wet spring day in Paris. Trees glistened with raindrops. Under a black umbrella, Pierre hurried along the slippery pavement. He was eager to get home. Lately, he and Marie never seemed to have enough time for themselves. After winning the Nobel Prize, they were very much in demand. There were constant requests to write articles or to make speeches.

Pierre started to cross a street that had been flooded by the rain. Head down, he did not notice a horse-drawn wagon hurtling toward him. People began shouting at him to be careful. The driver of the wagon jerked frantically on the horses' reins. But it was too late.

Pierre slipped and lost his balance. He tumbled under the wheels of the wagon. An instant later, he was dead.

Pierre Curie died on April 19, 1906. He was only forty-seven years old.

When the news of the accident was brought to Marie, she stood speechless. She simply could not believe that her husband had been killed. It was a terrible blow. What would she do without him?

Now Marie was a widow at thirty-nine. She had two little girls to look after. In the dark days that followed, she struggled to remain calm. It was important to carry on. In her memory, Marie could still hear Pierre's words. "Remember, Marie," he had told her, "if one of us were missing, the one who is left will go on alone...for the sake of the one who is gone...as well as for the sake of science!"

Marie never dreamed that they would lose each other so soon. However, she would devote all her energy to continue the work they had started together.

In spite of her courage, Marie felt that a part of her was gone. After Pierre's death, the French government offered Marie and her daughters a pension. For the rest of their lives, they would be given money to live on. Marie decided to turn down the pension. She was determined to earn her own living, as she had always done.

She persuaded the Sorbonne to give her Pierre's old position. Although Marie was a world-famous scientist, her getting the job was remarkable. No woman had ever before been hired for such a position. So in 1906, Marie became the first woman professor at the university.

In the years that followed, it was necessary for Marie to juggle her career and her family. As was her lifelong habit, she drove herself. To honor her husband, she founded the Curie Institute of Radium.

The new lab was devoted to the study of radioactivity.

In 1911, Marie won the Nobel Prize again. This time, it was the Nobel Prize in chemistry. It was awarded to Marie for her discovery of radium and polonium. The publicity was overwhelming.

Marie wanted more time to spend with her children. It is not surprising that she felt special concern about their education. Her older daughter, Irène, reminded Marie of herself. Even as a very young child, Irène began to show a strong interest in science. Naturally, this pleased her mother greatly.

In 1914, World War I began. Europe was at war, and the French people were plunged into a nightmare. By this time, Marie considered France her home. When the war started, she offered her help. The second Nobel award had again brought Marie a large sum of money. She decided to donate the prize money to the French government.

Marie believed that she could put her scientific knowledge to use. In 1895, Wilhelm Roentgen had discovered X rays. X rays could be used by doctors to locate injuries inside the body.

But the use of X rays was very limited. Few hospitals had X-ray equipment. For this reason, no one thought of using X rays on the wounded soldiers at the fighting front. As a result, many of the wounded died. Marie realized that the use of X rays would save soldiers' lives.

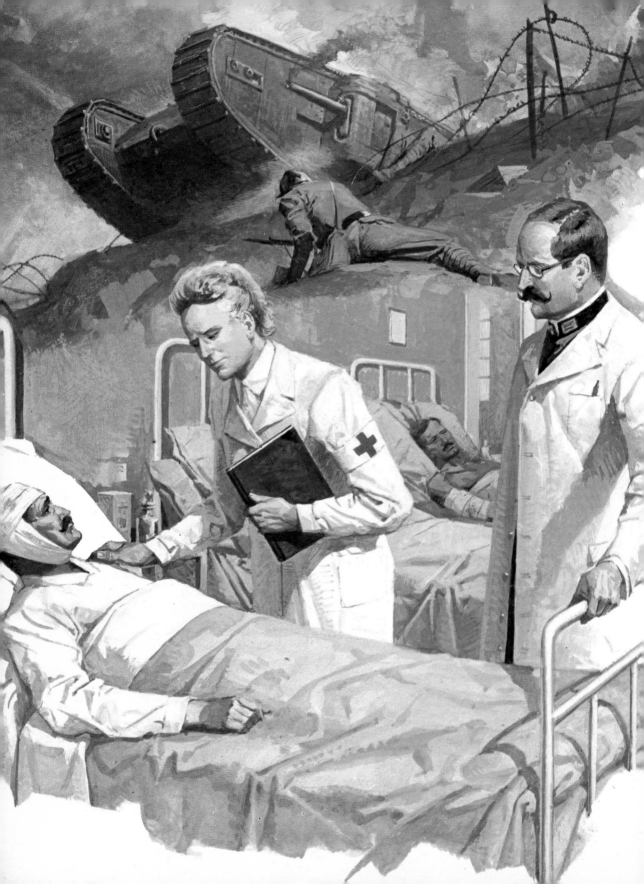

The problem was how to get the X-ray equipment to the front lines. Marie thought of building X-ray equipment that could be mounted on trucks and sent to the front.

That was not all Marie did. Assisted by Irène, who was seventeen, Marie trained 150 nurses in the use of the X-ray equipment. Sometimes the number of trained nurses was just not large enough. Then Marie and Irène would travel to the front and operate the equipment themselves. Their brave efforts saved many lives.

November 1918 was a proud and joyous time for Marie. The war finally ended. A few days later, the French government honored Marie and Irène. They received the Medal of Courage for their work in caring for the wounded. During the very same month, Marie's native country won its liberty at last. The Republic of Poland was declared on November 3, 1918.

After the war, Marie continued to work and to win honors. Sixteen-hour days were not uncommon. She was the first woman to be elected to the French Academy of Medicine. To help the cause of world peace, she served many organizations, including the League of Nations. She also founded the Marie Sklodowska-Curie Institute of Radium in Warsaw. Her sister Bronya became its director.

In 1920, Marie was fifty-three years old—and she had become ill. She was not a person who talked

about her suffering. Indeed, for a long time she had
tried to ignore her feelings of fatigue and dizziness.

Before the war, she had been forced to
undergo a serious operation on her kidneys. Now she
could not ignore the fact that something even more
terrible was happening. It was becoming hard for
her to read. Her sight seemed to be fading. She was
almost blind. It could not be kept a secret any
longer. In 1923, Marie had four eye operations.
Fortunately, most of her vision was restored.

During the 1920s, mysterious ailments began
to trouble Marie. Her symptoms puzzled the doctors.

Daily, she grew weaker. Finally, they decided that her sickness was similar to pernicious anemia, a disease that affects the blood cells. In those days, there was no known cure. Today it's known that Marie had leukemia.

Marie's illness was caused by radium poisoning. The many years of handling radioactive elements had done their damage. Today it is well known that radium can cause cancer and radiation sickness. But at that time, the effects of radiation were not yet known.

Marie was happy to see that Irène had followed in her footsteps. In 1926, Irène married a physicist, Frédéric Joliot. Frédéric was so honored to be entering the Curie family that he changed his last name to Joliot-Curie. Like Marie and Pierre, Irène and Frédéric also did research together. Their special subject was radioactive chemical elements.

In 1935, Irène and Frédéric Joliot-Curie received the Nobel Prize in chemistry. It was the first time that two generations of the same family had such an honor.

But Marie Curie did not have the joy of seeing her daughter and son-in-law receive the award. She died on July 4, 1934, at the age of sixty-six.

Throughout her life, Marie Curie was constant in her service to others. She is, along with her husband Pierre, one of the most important and humane figures in the history of science.

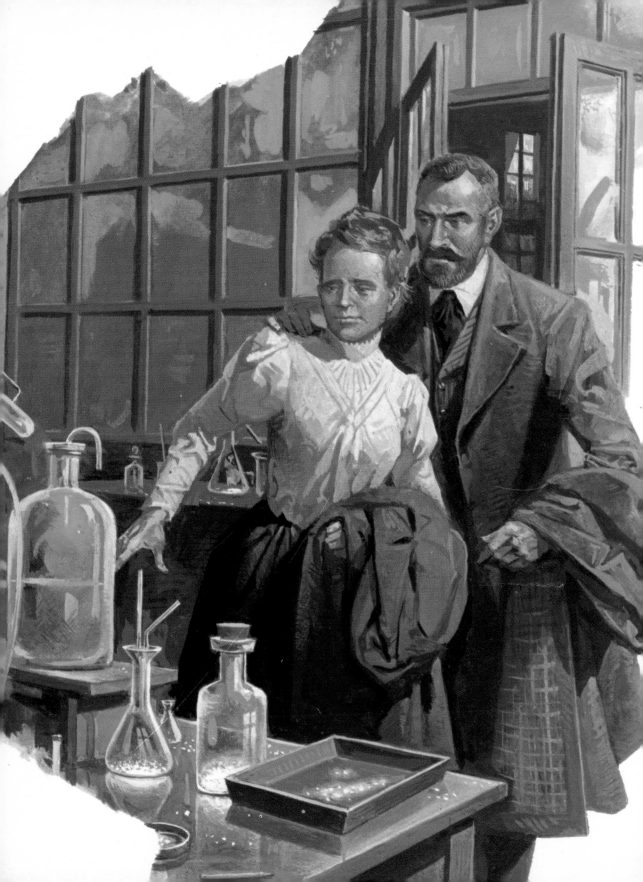

Marie Curie's Place in the Century of Science

ach period of history makes its special contribution to human knowledge. Today, the nineteenth century is remembered as "The Century of Science." And it was indeed a golden age of science.

A flood of new ideas emerged and many important discoveries were made. They revolutionized the way in which people live.

In the nineteenth century, giant leaps were taken in almost every area of science—chemistry, physics, biology, and medicine. New forms of transportation were devised. For the first time, people were able to communicate with one another over long distances. There were many exciting inventions in the fields of optics and photography, as well. Without these remarkable discoveries, life in the twentieth century would be much different.

Many great people were responsible for the enormous changes that took place. In the early 1800s, George Stephenson built the first steam locomotive. In 1837, Samuel Morse invented the wire telegraph. Two years later, Louis-Jacques Daguerre put together a camera—and photography was born.

Not long after, the rotary printing press was invented. Next came dynamite, produced by Alfred Nobel in 1867. Thomas Alva Edison turned on the first electric light bulb in 1879. A few years later, the internal combustion engine was invented.

In the 1880s, great advances were made in conquering diseases. The bacilli of tuberculosis, cholera, and diphtheria were discovered.

The century drew to a close with Roentgen discovering X rays in 1895. That same year, the Lumière brothers invented cinematography, which would make motion pictures possible.

Many great thinkers lived and worked in the nineteenth century. But one woman and one man towered above all the others. Marie and Pierre Curie are the best-known wife-and-husband team in the history of science.

The Curies were two exceptional people who dedicated their lives to science. They were courageous and determined individuals. In spite of a severe lack of money, they carried out their investigations over many, many years. The Curies were eventually honored for their discoveries of polonium and radium. It was then that the story of these two scientists became known throughout the world.

Marie Curie is best remembered for her brilliant mind. Her regard for others and her sense of responsibility also made her very special.

Throughout World War I, she worked on the application of X rays for medical diagnosis. She put her knowledge at the service of medicine, by organizing the French army's radiology services. Her work saved the lives of thousands of soldiers.

After the war, most of her research was on the use of radioactive substances in the treatment of illness.

Marie Curie left a legacy of important discoveries for future generations of scientists. She also was a person of very strong character. Throughout her life she tried to serve her fellow human beings. Her work helped to improve the lives of us all.

Radiotherapy

X rays, radium, and radioactive substances are used in medicine for therapeutic and diagnostic purposes. For instance, radium and radon—a radioactive gas derived from radium—are used in the treatment of tumors. They destroy the diseased tissues, whenever it is impossible or inadvisable to intervene surgically, and when other medical treatments are unsuccessful.

Radioactive cobalt is used for tumors found in deep tissues. Thanks to a device called a "cobalt bomb," the cobalt can be aimed directly at the diseased area.

X rays, a kind of invisible natural energy that can make an imprint on a film or negative, are used in radiology. Since the various tissues in the body (bones, teeth, soft tissues, muscles, cartilage, and so on) absorb the rays in varying amounts, the negatives show the different areas as lighter or darker shadows.

Soft tissues absorb practically no rays, but they can be photographed with the aid of contrasting substances that make the organ opaque and, therefore, visible to the X rays.

Radioscopy, a special radiological technique, allows the image of internal organs to be projected onto a fluorescent screen. Thus, a physician can quickly examine an area of the body and study its movements (such as, heart beat, respiratory movements).

Scintigraphy is another diagnostic tool. This technique uses radioisotopes—radioactive particles.

Such particles are introduced into the patient's body. Then, the radioactive concentration is absorbed by the organs to be examined and can then be measured. Conclusions about the condition of the organs can thus be formulated.

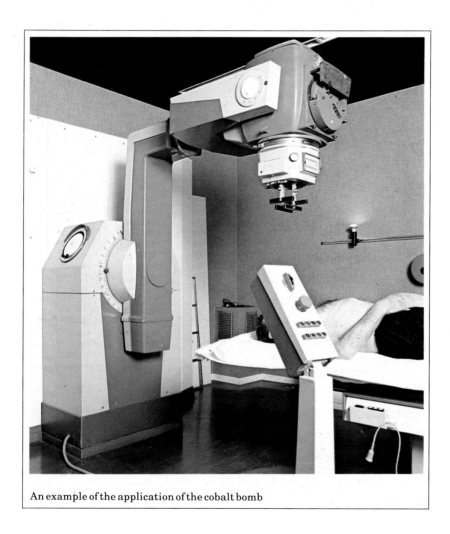

An example of the application of the cobalt bomb

Radioactive Weapons

Following Irène and Frédéric Joliot-Curie's discovery of artificial radioactivity—after which they won the Nobel Prize in chemistry—the two became very interested in studying the nucleus of the atom. Eventually, Frédéric proved that it was possible to create atomic energy.

Despite the Joliot-Curies' commitment to using atomic energy for peaceful purposes, Frédéric's experiments helped scientists to develop the atomic bomb—the dreadful weapon used in World War II.

When a heavy atom—such as an atom of uranium—is bombarded, an immeasurable amount of energy is released. In 1939, it was discovered that uranium atoms could be divided into two parts, causing a "chain reaction." This splitting of atoms, called nuclear fission, is the basis of atomic power. An enormous amount of energy can be generated by subjecting a ton of uranium to this process.

On August 6, 1945, at 9:15 A.M., the United States dropped an atomic bomb on Hiroshima, Japan. Three days later, at 12:01 A.M., another American bomber dropped an atomic bomb on Nagasaki, Japan. The fission, thermic, and radioactive effects of the atomic bomb were catastrophic. A few seconds after the explosion, which consisted of an intensely bright ball of fire, a white "mushroom cloud," several miles in height, appeared. It dissolved in a few hours. A violent jet of air erupted, and a strong wind converged on the epicenter of the explosion. The wind, accompanied by intermittent rain, ceased in a few hours. Within a square mile of the epicenter, all buildings were destroyed. Ninety persons out of one hundred were killed. Short circuits, fires, and gas leaks occurred within three square miles.

The devastating effects of the bomb on people were even more horrifying. The "acute radiation syndrome" caused vomiting, fever, general weakness, and, almost invariably, death.

Thermonuclear explosion in Bikini, Marshall Islands

Marie Curie and the Political Rights of Women

During the debate about passing the law granting the right to vote to Frenchwomen, Senator Bruguir intervened on July 7, 1932, reminding everyone

Feminist movement in England—women writing propaganda in favor of voting rights for women

that the "feminists" had the support of famous women such as Marie Curie, who belonged to the intellectual elite. Another senator, Barthou, sharply contradicted him.

When Marie Curie found out about the dispute between the two senators, she proceeded to clarify her position in a letter addressed to Louis Marin, president of the group that favored women's suffrage.

Mr. President:

I have been informed that during the debate about the women's vote (meeting of July 7, 1932), my name was mentioned, and an opinion opposed to granting women the right to vote was attributed to me. This, of course, was a misunderstanding. Actually, I tend to abstain from any political issue— be it the case in question or any other case— if it is not related to science. I will not give my opinion on the procedures to be followed; however, I think the principle of conferring political rights upon women is essentially just and must be recognized.

I would appreciate it, Mr. President, if you would let the Senate know about the contents of this letter.

Best regards.
Marie Curie

The Nobel Prize

Alfred Bernhard Nobel was born in Stockholm in 1833. He is famous for having invented dynamite, an explosive material that is still in use, and that is very similar to gunpowder, but does not produce smoke. Thanks to his patents and to the oil fields he acquired in Baku, the Swedish chemist made an enormous fortune. On November 27, 1895, he bequeathed his entire fortune to a foundation (Nobelstiftelsen) that would award five prizes every year to those who "offered their services to humanity" in the fields of chemistry, physics, medicine, and physiology, literature, and friendly relations between peoples.

Nobel died, in 1896, in San Remo. He is still remembered for the prestigious international prize that bears his name. Since 1901, the Nobel Foundation has awarded the five annual prizes—in chemistry, physics, medicine, literature, and peace—to those who merit them.

Medal given to Nobel Prize winners.
On the back of the medal is the image
of Alfred Nobel.

HISTORICAL CHRONOLOGY

Life of Marie Curie	Historical and Cultural Events
1867 November 7—Manya Sklodowska is born in Warsaw.	**1867** Nobel invents dynamite.
	1869 Lesseps completes the opening of the Suez Canal. Mendeleev conceives the periodic table of chemical elements.
	1871 Foundation of the German Empire. Meucci patents the telephone.
1873 Manya's sister Zosia dies of typhus at age fourteen.	

Warsaw—view of the National Palace—1872 engraving

Inauguration of the Suez Canal—contemporary illustration

Life of Marie Curie	Historical and Cultural Events
1876 Manya's mother dies of tuberculosis.	**1876** Bell and Gray start to produce telephones on a large scale.
	1878 Thomas Edison invents the phonograph.
	1879 Edison makes the first light bulb.
	1881 Inauguration of Gottardo's Gallery. Siemens constructs the first electronic tramway.
	1882 The Triple Alliance of Germany, Austria, and Hungary is formed. Koch discovers the bacillus of tuberculosis.
	1885 Koch discovers the bacillus of cholera. Benz and Daimler construct a car with an internal combustion engine.

Proclamation of the German Empire in Versailles

Experiencing the telephone at the Palazzo Marino, in Milan—nineteenth-century engraving

Life of Marie Curie	Historical and Cultural Events
	1889 The Eiffel Tower is constructed for the World's Fair held in Paris.
1891 Manya leaves Warsaw for Paris to study at the Sorbonne University. She changes her name to Marie.	
	1892 Toulouse-Lautrec creates a sign for the Moulin Rouge, which is a masterpiece of "Art Nouveau" and, at the same time, the first advertising sign.

Eiffel Tower, Paris—constructed for the 1889 World's Fair

Henri Toulouse-Lautrec—advertising sign for the Moulin Rouge

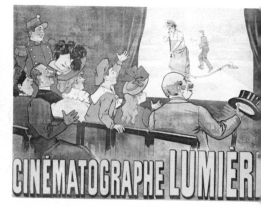

A. Anzolle—advertising sign for the film *The Wet Gardener*

Life of Marie Curie	Historical and Cultural Events
1893 Marie gets a degree in physics.	**1893** Diesel perfects an engine that is named after him.
1894 Marie gets a degree in mathematics.	
1895 Marie Sklodowska marries Pierre Curie.	**1895** Roentgen discovers X rays. Lumière invents cinematography.
1897 Irène is born to Marie and Pierre Curie.	**1897** Marconi invents the wireless telegraph.
1898 Marie and Pierre Curie discover polonium and radium.	

First Fiat model, 3-1/2 HP, conceived by the engineer A. Faccioli

The first flight of the Wright brothers in their "flying machine"

Life of Marie Curie	Historical and Cultural Events
	1899 The first Fiat car is produced.
	1900 Zeppelin constructs the dirigible.
1902 Marie Curie's father dies. The Curies' second child dies shortly after birth.	**1902** Marconi unites Italy and the United States through the wireless telegraph.
1903 Marie gets a degree in physics from the Sorbonne University. Marie and Pierre Curie win the Nobel Prize in physics.	**1903** First flight by the Wright brothers.

Assassination of Archduke Francis Ferdinand—La Domenica del Corriere

Life of Marie Curie	Historical and Cultural Events
1904 Eve, Marie and Pierre Curie's daughter, is born.	
	1905 Einstein formulates the theory of relativity.
1906 Pierre Curie is hit by a carriage and dies.	**1906** Theodore Roosevelt, President of the United States, wins the Nobel Peace Prize.
1911 Marie Curie wins the Nobel Prize in chemistry.	

Crowning of Czar Nicholas II—
illustration of the time

Emiliano Zapata—mosaic by Diego Rivera

Life of Marie Curie	Historical and Cultural Events
	1914 Archduke Francis Ferdinand of Austria is assassinated in Sarajevo. World War I breaks out.
	1916 Einstein formulates the general theory of relativity.
	1917 Nicholas II abdicates—Russian Revolution.
1918 The French government confers the Medal of Courage to Marie and Irène Curie for their work during the war.	**1918** End of World War I. Independence of Poland, Czechoslovakia, Hungary, and Yugoslavia.
	1919 Zapata—the great Mexican revolutionary chief—is assassinated after having fought for agrarian reform.

Benito Mussolini
with King
Victor Emmanuel III

Life of Marie Curie	Historical and Cultural Events
1921 President Harding gives Marie Curie a gram of radium.	
1922 Marie Curie is elected member of the French Academy of Medicine.	**1922** Benito Mussolini takes over the government of Italy; advent of fascism in Italy.
1925 Marie places the foundation stone for the Radium Institute in Warsaw.	
1926 Irène Curie marries Frédéric Joliot.	**1926** Grazia Deledda wins the Nobel Prize in literature.
	1928 First sound film— *The Jazz Singer*—is produced in the United States.
	1929 U.S. economic crisis and collapse of the Stock Exchange.

Writer Grazia Deledda

Life of Marie Curie	Historical and Cultural Events
	1933 Nazism starts in Germany with Hitler. First electronic microscope.
1934 Irène and Frédéric Joliot-Curie obtain a radioactive isotope of phosphorus in the lab. July 4—Marie Curie dies of leukemia, due to prolonged exposure to radiation.	
	1938 Enrico Fermi wins the Nobel Prize for having demonstrated the presence of new radioactive elements produced by neutron bombardment.
	1939 Penicillin—already discovered by Fleming in 1928—is used as an antibiotic.

Portrait of Sir A. Fleming, thought to be by T. C. Dugdale

BOOKS FOR FURTHER READING

Marie Curie by Angela Bull, Hamish Hamilton, 1986.

Marie Curie by Edwina Conner, Watts, 1987.

Marie Curie by Louis Sabin, Troll Associates, 1985.

Marie Curie by Ann Steinke, Barron, 1987.

Marie Curie: Brave Scientist by Keith Brandt, Troll Associates, 1983.

Marie Curie: Pioneer Physicist by Carol Green, Children's Press, 1984.

Marie Curie: The Polish Scientist Who Discovered Radium and Its Life-Saving Properties by Beverly Birch, Gareth Stevens, 1988.

INDEX